The Enlightened Empath

A Comprehensive Guide to Emotional Healing for Highly Sensitive People

William E. Joyce

Table of Contents

Introduction 1

Chapter 1: The Basics 3

    What is an empath? 3

    Common traits 5

        High sensitivity 5

        Understanding 6

        Need to be alone 7

        Confusion 8

        Strong intuition 9

        They easily attract people 10

        They sometimes feel drained 11

    Are you an empath? 12

    How to develop empathy 13

        Use your feelings 13

        Meditation 14

        Connect with people 14

        Spend time in solitude 14

        Focus on other people 15

Chapter 2: Dealing With People 17

    How to deal with difficult people 17

    Building ideal relationships 19

    Finding the 'one' for you 20

Chapter 3: Best Practices 23

    Introspection 23

Meditation 25
    Meditation on the breath 27
    Butterfly effect 28
    White light 30
    Connect 31
    Blessing and forgiveness 32
    Waterfall technique 34
    Bubble shield 35
    Sensing 36

Mindfulness 37

Yoga 38

Relaxation 40

Chapter 4: Do's and Don'ts 45

Dos 45
    Write a journal 45
    Mingle with positive people 47
    Continuous practice 48
    Positive thinking 49
    Know who you are 51
    Take a break 52

Don'ts 53
    Do not lie to yourself 53
    Do not give up 55
    Do not entertain negative thoughts 56
    Do not let people change who you are 58
    Do not think of your ability as a curse 59

Conclusion 61

© **Copyright 2018 by Candere Publishing Company - All rights reserved.**

The transmission, duplication, or reproduction of any of the following work including specific information will be considered an illegal act irrespective of whether it is done electronically or in print. This extends to creating a secondary or tertiary copy of the work or a recorded copy and is only allowed with the express written consent from the Publisher. All additional rights reserved.

The information in the following pages is broadly considered to be a truthful and accurate account of facts, and as such any inattention, use, or misuse of the information in question by the reader will render any resulting actions solely under their purview. There are no scenarios in which the publisher or the original author of this work can be, in any fashion, deemed liable for any hardship or damages that may befall them after undertaking information described herein. The author does not take any responsibility for inaccuracies, omissions, or errors which may be found therein.

Additionally, the information in the following pages is intended only for informational purposes and should thus be thought of as universal. As befitting its nature, it is presented without assurance regarding its prolonged validity or interim quality. The author of this work is not responsible for any loss, damage, or inconvenience caused as a result of reliance on information as published on, or linked, to this book.

The author of this book has taken careful measures to share vital information about the subject. May its readers acquire the right knowledge, wisdom, inspiration, and succeed.

Introduction

Congratulations on downloading this book and thank you for doing so.

The following chapters will teach you everything that you need to know about empathy, as well as how you can effectively deal with it:

- Chapter 1 talks about the basics of empathy to give you a good foundation and understanding of what being an empath really means

- Chapter 2 teaches how you should deal with people, and how you can create ideal relationships

- Chapter 3 discusses the best practices that you should observe to help you gain mastery over your empathic ability

- Chapter 4 lays down the 'dos' and 'don'ts' of being an empath.

There are plenty of books on this subject on the market, so thanks again for choosing this one! Every effort was made to ensure it is full of as much useful information as possible. Please enjoy!

Chapter 1:
The Basics

What is an empath?

The term 'empath' refers to a person who can feel what other people feel. This ability is called empathy. Empaths are very sensitive to subtle energies and emotions. If left undeveloped, empaths can easily confuse other people's emotions as their own, and this can be a problem in the long run. If you think that you have empathic abilities, then you should learn how to develop and work with it. Empaths who do not work on their ability usually end up thinking that their ability is a curse. However, this is not true. In fact, empathic abilities are a wonderful gift, especially if you know how to use it properly and live harmoniously with it.

So, what does it mean to feel how other people feel? Well, it can be confusing if you are not used to having this ability. This is why many empaths out there think that their gift is more of a curse than a blessing. A true and well-trained empath is able to distinguish their own emotions from the emotions of other people. They are also capable of connecting to other people on a more intimate level since they can understand people easily. An empath can also read people very well since they can feel them, and feelings do not lie. As you can see, there are many benefits of being an empath. In the beginning, you might have trouble learning how you're supposed to use your ability, but once you learn how to control it, then you will start to appreciate its beauty, and that is the time when you will be happy for being an empath.

However, if this ability is left uncontrolled, then certain problems may arise. One of the common problems of being an empath is that you can get easily hurt or insulted. This is because you are very sensitive, which makes you easily offended. Another common problem is being confused as to who you really are. There are times when you are so sensitive that you can no longer distinguish the emotions of other people from your own. This is why part of your training is knowing how to identify your own emotions from others.

So, what makes an empath? In spirituality, empathy occurs when you have a well-developed heart *chakra*. What is the heart *chakra*? It refers to the *chakra* that is located in the middle of your chest. It is one of the 7 main *chakras* of the body. A *chakra* is also referred to as a spinning wheel. If the physical body has vital organs, then the immaterial body has *chakras* or energy centers. *Chakras* ensure the free flow of energy in your body that keeps you alive. By dealing with empathy, you will have to work on your heart chakra because it is the center of universal love and emotions. Your heart *chakra* is located in the center of your chest, and it has a green color.

Some people are born as natural empaths while others acquire and develop this ability at some point in their life. Regardless of the reason, the important thing is whether or not you have an empathic ability. If you do not have this ability, then it is up to you to decide whether you want to learn it, or if you want to just stay as you are. However, if you do have empathy, then it is strongly suggested that you learn and discover more about this wonderful gift that you have.

Common traits

High sensitivity

Empaths are highly sensitive people. This is probably the number one trait of an empath. If left uncontrolled, then this can be a problem in the sense that you can get easily offended by people since you are overly sensitive to the point that even a simple joke can make you feel insulted or offended.

If you notice that you are more sensitive than others, then there is a good chance that you are an empath. Take note that this sensitivity is not limited to yourself, but it is also about being sensitive to how other people feel. If you easily sympathize with people, then there is a good chance that you have an empathic ability.

Being able to feel people's intentions is often considered a sign that you have heightened sensitivity. Do you happen to have this gut feeling when somebody has a good or bad intention? This is a sure sign that you are an empath. Empathy enables you to feel and see beyond the things in front of you. This is how you get to connect with people on a much deeper level. This high sensitivity is not something that you do intentionally, but it should be something that comes naturally to you. Hence, you should be able to feel other people's energies without forcing yourself to do so.

Although being highly sensitive is the most common trait of an empath, it should be noted that it is also the most problematic part of being an empath. If you do not learn to control your ability, this heightened sensitivity can make you feel terrible to the point that a slight offense can hurt you and make you feel gravely offended. It can also make you feel confused in such a way that you can no longer distinguish your emotions from the people around you.

Understanding

Since empaths can feel how other people truly feel, they know how to understand others easily. People usually voice out how they feel, but only a few can truly comprehend their emotions. This is because emotions are not that easy to be put into words.

Moreover, not everyone is capable of enough understanding. Empaths do not just understand what you tell them, but they also sympathize with you. If you are an empath, then you know that this means more than having the intellect to understand a particular emotion. It is about directly feeling how other people feel. Sometimes you may even feel the emotion more strongly than the person who is actually feeling it. This is because you are more sensitive than most people, and you get to experience things more intimately.

If you are an empath, then you will certainly have a very understanding nature. In fact, people do not even have to explain to you how they feel because you can feel it directly as if you were that other person. Empaths understand that emotions can be a lot stronger than the rational mind. They also know that not all emotions are logical. Sometimes people can feel good or bad for no reason. Empaths are aware of how the quality of the energies around us can change. Since they can see and feel the bigger picture, they tend to be more understanding.

As you may already know, being understanding is important in any relationship. In fact, it is the lack of understanding that ruins most relationships. This is why empaths are good at building positive relationships and have no problem maintaining them. If you are an empath, chances are that you can understand another person more deeply.

In fact, it is not rare for empaths to understand someone more deeply than that person understands themselves. This level of understanding is the reason why empaths tend to treat everyone kindly. However, a common problem empaths have is that they are very understanding of others, but they are not being treated with the same level of understanding. After all, not everyone is an empath. This is something that you need to understand and even get used to. Do not expect people to understand you the way you understand others. Again, the people around you are probably not empaths like yourself, so do not feel bad when people fail to sympathize with you.

Need to be alone

Do you sometimes have this feeling, almost like a need, to be alone and spend some time in solitude? This is one of the main signs of being an empath. Empaths need time to be alone every now and then. By spending time alone with yourself, you can remove or at least lessen your attachments to external things. It is also a good way to recover your self-identity after being exposed to different energies and emotions around you.

It is an excellent opportunity for you to find yourself and balance your being.

This desire to be alone, to have solitude does not happen all of the time, but if you are an empath, you will surely experience it every now and then, especially after being exposed to many people. This is true especially if you are exposed to negative people. Being alone is a natural way to release all the tensions in your life that you have absorbed from others. If you feel like you're being overcome or controlled by emotions, it is strongly advised that you take a step back away from everyone and spend some time alone. Empaths need time to be alone without being influenced by any external force. This is a good chance for them to reflect on their experiences and think more clearly.

Confusion

If you do not learn to control your empathic ability, it will be easy for you get confused. This is true especially when you have mixed emotions coming from different people. It is not unusual for untrained empaths to confuse other people's emotions as their own. The best way to deal with confusion is to take a step back and spend time in solitude as we have already discussed. Indeed, it can be confusing especially when you get exposed to the emotions of different people. It is important for you to have a good sense of who you are. This will help you distinguish the real you from the energies around you. Do not worry, you will learn powerful exercises later in the book, that will teach you how to effectively deal with confusion.

Confusion arises when you are exposed so much to the energies of others to the point that you think of them as your own. As an empath, you need to learn to control how much you absorb other people's energies, as well as to distinguish your own energy from others.

Remember that when you feel confused, the best thing that you should do is to spend time alone with yourself. The more that you isolate yourself from others, the more easily you can free yourself from the energies of those around you. Once you withdraw yourself into isolation, you will notice that the confusion tends to decrease, and then gradually it will completely disappear. However, it is worth mentioning that, for this to be effective, you must also free your mind and not allow it to hold on to the energies of other people. This is an excellent time for you to practice meditation and other relaxation techniques.

Do not be afraid if you ever feel confused. If you are an empath, then being confused is normal. What you need to do is to learn how to effectively deal with the different energies around you and live in harmony with them.

Strong intuition

Empaths are also known for having a strong intuition. This is because as an empath, you are not just open to emotions, but you are open to all subtle energies. You are sensitive to energies that most people do not even recognize. Although you cannot see these energies, you can feel them. And, as you already know, feelings do not lie. This is also why some experts prefer to be empathic than being clairvoyant.

Before we go any further, let us first discuss what the intuition is. So, what is intuition? The intuition refers to the ability to know something without any logical explanation. For example, as an empath, you may find it easy to feel if a particular person is good or bad. It is also worth noting that the ability to be empathic is also connected with the *Ajna chakra*. What is the *Ajna chakra*? It is the sixth chakra, and it has an indigo color. It is more commonly referred to as the 'third eye chakra.' It is the seat of intuition. Contrary to what others believe, the exact location of the *Ajna chakra* is right in the middle of the eyebrows. If you are familiar with people who rely on their gut feeling, then that is an exercise of the intuition. However, it should be noted that most people are no longer in touch with subtle energies. In fact, they do not even understand the language of intuition, which explains why their intuition fails. The truth is, intuition never fails. Rather, it is how a person interprets their intuition is where the mistake happens. True empaths know that they can rely on their intuition. They do not just know things, but they also feel things. It should be noted that everything is made of energy, physical things, as well as thoughts and emotions, are all energies. If you notice that you have a strong sense of intuition based on how you feel, then there is a good chance that you might be an empath.

They easily attract people

Since empaths are very understanding and are capable of connecting with people on a deeper level, they tend to attract people easily. After all, who would not want to talk with someone who understands you even better than yourself? These days, it is rare to find someone who could understand how you feel. People have become used to shutting out their

Chapter 1: The Basics

feelings to give more emphasis to logical thoughts. An empath usually makes people feel more natural and true. There is a sense of trust and openness since you know that you are being understood. However, the drawback here is that empaths normally attract lots of negative people. This is because empaths understand negative people, and they even extend more kindness to them than others. While most people will just run away from a negative person, an empath may find some good in that person and even spend more time with them. Of course, this is a matter of personal preference. However, since an empath has a deeper sense of understanding when it comes to people, they tend to sympathize better and have more patience when dealing with difficult people. However, this does not mean that this is easy. As an empath, you must be prepared for this.

They sometimes feel drained

Do you sometimes feel like you're out of energy, especially after you're done dealing with a negative person? Well, this level of sensitivity is normally attributed to empaths. Another clear sign of empathy is that you feel drained after you were exposed to a crowd, especially if you met difficult people. Negative people are like parasites. They tend to draw and suck in the positive energy of empaths. This is why if you are an empath, you need to learn certain protective measures to avoid being drained of energy. Remember that negative energies cling to positive energies. This is because negative energies have a lower vibration and want to achieve a higher vibration. To do this, negative energies have to cling and absorb positive energies. This is also called 'energy vampirism.' As an empath, you need to be aware of this so you can protect yourself from parasites. Being drained means that you have lost energy. Avoid negativity because negative energies will drain you of positive energy. Therefore, it is strongly suggested that you only stick to positive people and stay away from difficult people.

Now, there are those who might ask, "Can this be avoided?" The answer is yes. Also, even if you get drained, there are measures that you can do to recover the lost energy and free yourself from negativity. All this will be discussed in chapter 3 of this book. For now, it is good to have knowledge of the basics of being an empath. Do not forget that knowledge is power. The more that you understand what empathy is, the more that you can exercise control over it.

Are you an empath?

So, are you an empath? By now, you should already have a good idea of the signs of being an empath. If you think that you are probably an empath, then good for you. Why? Because empathy is a gift, provided you learn how to control it.

Although it is true that there are empaths who hate their gift, the truth is that you will start to appreciate it as a blessing once you know how to control it instead of the other way around. Unfortunately, many empaths end up being controlled by their ability. This is why you need to learn more about it and start doing effective practices like meditation so you can learn how to use your ability properly.

Since you are reading this book, you are probably another empath who may be having issues with your ability. Just relax

Chapter 1: The Basics

and keep on reading and remember not to worry because you possess a wonderful gift, and you simply have to learn how to use it well.

There are two things that you need to do: First, you need to acquire the right knowledge to better understand the ability that you have. Second, you need to take the necessary actions to put your empathic ability under your control. This book will provide you with the right knowledge. It is up to you to put your newfound knowledge into actual practice.

Most people do not understand what an empath is, so do not feel bad if you feel like nobody understands you. After all, there are only a few empaths out there, and still, fewer are those who have mastery and control over their ability.

How to develop empathy

The truth is, everybody can be an empath. Yes, you can be an empath. Also, even if you are already an empath, you can still develop and improve your empathic ability. So, how do you develop (or become) an empath? Well, here are some things that you can do:

Use your feelings

Before you understand how other people feel, you should first get used to the language of emotions. Of course, the best way to do this is by paying attention and observing your own emotions. Get used to listening to your feelings. Do not be too logical. Learn to acknowledge your emotions and listen to them. The more that you do this, the more that you will get used to understanding emotions. In the beginning, you might feel a bit uncomfortable with this exercise, but you will soon get used to it.

Meditation

Practicing meditation is one of the best ways to develop empathy. Regularly practicing meditation is an effective way to strengthen the *chakras* of the body, including the *chakras* responsible for empathic abilities. If you want to master your ability to show empathy, then the practice of meditation is a must.

Connect with people

Empathy is about connecting with people, specifically, with how they feel. To do this, you need to connect with people first. If you really want to learn empathy or develop empathy, you need to get used to connecting with different people. However, instead of just talking to them, focus more on listening to them. Do not just listen to their words, but try to focus on their feelings. Use the power of your intention to feel how they feel. Now, do not expect this experience to be always pleasant. From time to time, you may have to deal with negative people. Just be patient and always exercise kindness.

Spend time in solitude

Solitude is important to empaths. Every now and then you should spend some time alone by yourself and observe how you feel. Now, go out and spend time with people and compare the difference. You will see how other people have an effect on how you feel. For empaths, spending time in solitude is a regular thing. You will definitely need to give yourself some alone time every now and then.

Focus on other people

You should understand that empathy is not about you, but it is more about other people, specifically their feelings. So, if you want to learn how to be an empath, you should stop focusing on yourself and start being interested in other people.

It is also worth noting that the practices in chapter 3 of this book are also excellent ways to develop empathy.

Here is another question: "Is it possible to reduce one's empathic abilities after you have acquired it?" The answer to this question is no. However, it is possible to decrease the power of your empathic ability. This usually happens when you stop doing the practices which will be discussed later in this book. However, the danger here is that your ability may start to gain control over you instead of the other way around. You need to realize that you cannot escape your gift. Instead of despising it, you should learn to understand it.

If you do, you will soon start to see it as a blessing. Empathy gives you the power to feel and understand how other people feel. However, as the saying goes, "With great power comes great responsibility." You should be responsible enough to learn how to control your ability so that you can use it properly and effectively.

Chapter 2: Dealing With People

How to deal with difficult people

As an empath, a common problem is learning how to deal with difficult people. In fact, even if you are not an empath, getting along with difficult people is quite a challenge. It is all the more challenging if you can be empathic. Difficult people tend to be negative, obnoxious, and loud people.

Unfortunately, some people are so insensitive that they tend to offend other people and yet, they think there's nothing wrong with what they doing. If you are an empath, you need to protect yourself from negative people. If you are not yet in control of your ability, it is advised that you stay away from difficult people. It is simply not that easy to deal with them. However, the truth is, you cannot always avoid such situations. So, what do you do when you have to confront with difficult people?

The first thing that you need to remember is that you shouldn't allow yourself to get attached to them. You should not allow their words to affect you either. In line with their nature as difficult people, you can expect them to say something negative about almost anything. Keep in mind that no one can corrupt and hurt you without your consent.

Instead of seeing difficult people as simply rude and offensive people, realize that they are actually the best teachers in virtue and perfection. They are the ones who can really test your patience and other virtues.

You should also consider that negative people are not completely negative. They also have positive qualities. There is no one out there who is completely negative. Whenever you find yourself dealing with a difficult person, try to focus more on their positive qualities. Realize that people themselves are not negative, only some qualities that they have are. As the saying goes, "Hate the sin, love the sinner." In order not to be too affected, learn to separate the people from their bad behavior.

In the beginning, you may find it extremely challenging to get along with a difficult person. However, by becoming more understanding and by using your ability to sympathize with a person, you will know the right way to respond and deal with a negative person in a good manner. It is important to note that you should never allow negative people to change who you are. As an empath, it is easy for you to be influenced, but you should carefully choose what will influence you.

A common mistake is to hope for negative people to change. Although this is possible, it is something that is outside of your control. You cannot force another person to change. Change happens from the heart, so there is no way that you can force someone to change. Instead of expecting another person to change, you should learn to accept that person as they are. One of the best ways to get along with a difficult person is to simply accept them for who they are, including all their faults and imperfections. The key is to focus on the positive. Now, in case you cannot find the positive in another person, then try to find it in you. Never succumb to negativity.

Building ideal relationships

Everyone wants to have ideal relationships, empaths included. However, empaths may have issues with building those kinds of relationships, especially when they are not in control of their ability. Having empathy can be a serious problem if you fail to take control of it.

An ideal relationship should be mutual. This means that both parties in the relationship should be happy with the relationship. This is something that you cannot force. Indeed, even if you do not have any empathic ability, building an ideal relationship can be a challenge.

Your ability is something that you can use to create an ideal relationship. Remember that your empathic ability can help you understand another person more deeply. With empathy, you can connect with another person on a much deeper and meaningful level. A common mistake is to use empathy by focusing on yourself. You should realize as early as now that empathy is for other people. It is what you can use to connect and understand others more effectively. So, when learning how to use empathy, focus more on other people and less on yourself.

An ideal relationship requires two people to have a mutual understanding about one another. Even if you do everything correctly and still fail to find an ideal relationship, do not be discouraged. An important part of finding the ideal relationship is connecting with the right person. You can also use your empathic ability to help you identify the right people to connect with. As you can see, you can use your ability to help you find positive people and build a more meaningful relationship. Don't forget that an ideal relationship is also possible with a difficult person. After all, people can change, and even difficult people have something good about them. There are no hard and fast rules when it comes to building an ideal relationship. Just be open, use your ability properly, and see what works for you.

Finding the 'one' for you

Can you use your empathic ability to find your ideal lover? What does your partner have to be or do to make you feel better? Just do what you can use your ability to connect with positive people, you can also use it to find the right lover for you. However, do not expect this to be an easy task. You may have to go through a little trial and error to find the one for you. Using your ability will only help increase the chances of finding the right one, but there is no guarantee that you will find him or her. However, this is something that is definitely worth giving a try. The next time that you find yourself around people, use your ability and feel if there is any chance of having a more intimate relationship with anyone there. By doing so, you can save time and efforts instead of wasting them in a wrong relationship.

An ideal relationship would mean having a partner who would learn to get along well with you as an empath. Take note that every relationship should be mutual. Hence, both you and your partner should learn to adjust. Your partner does not need to be an empath, but he or she has to understand what you are going through as an empath. Your partner should also be sensitive about how you feel. This is not very hard to do, especially if you truly love each other. Although, it may take some time to make some adjustments.

Chapter 3: Best Practices

Let us now move on to the best practices that you should do if you are an empath. The problem with so many empaths is that they do nothing about their ability. It ends up controlling them instead of the other way around. If you want to take control of your empathic ability, then you need to take action.

Introspection

This is one of the most important things that you need to do if you can be empathic. Introspection is about examining and understanding yourself. The best way to do this is to spend some time in solitude where you are free to make reflections. It is also advised that you use a personal journal or diary where you can write down your thoughts and observations. Pay attention to how you feel and be honest with yourself. Also, observe your good and bad qualities. You should also take note of the thoughts that go on in your mind. This is about knowing yourself better. A common problem many empaths have is confusing other people's feelings with their own. By doing introspection, you will know yourself better, and you won't have problems distinguishing your own feelings and emotions from others.

It should be noted that, as an empath, you should practice introspection regularly. In fact, if you can, it is advised that you do it daily. If you are a very busy person, you can practice introspection in the evening before going to sleep. Think about what happened during the day and how you made good use of your ability. If you have committed some mistakes, then hold those thoughts for a moment and think about how you can avoid committing the same mistakes in the future. Learning about your empathic ability will help you learn more about yourself and how you can live life better.

When you practice introspection, remember to take as much time as needed. In fact, I would advise that you shouldn't pay attention to time at all. Keep in mind that this is about making reflections and learning, and this is definitely the process that you do not want to miss out on.

You can also practice introspection as you go through your day-to-day life. If you ever feel like you are being influenced by an external force, stop whatever it is that you are doing and examine yourself. Most of the time, by doing this, you will easily distinguish your own emotions from others. It should also be noted that when you do introspection, you have to be calm. You should see yourself from a different perspective without any bias or prejudice. This is why using a journal or diary is strongly advised. This will be discussed in more detail later in the book.

Of course, the goal of introspection is self-improvement. If you notice some things or qualities that you should change or need to be developed, then you must do something about it. Now, change is not exactly an easy thing to do. After all, it's difficult to change habits, including bad habits. And more so, if you replace them with good habits. The good news is that this is possible and that you can do it. It will just really take some time and efforts on your part, but it is nonetheless doable. When it comes to being an empath, then introspection should definitely be on your list of things to do.

Meditation

Meditation plays a very important role in being an empath. Before discussing the different meditation techniques, let us first discuss what meditation is, as well as the important points that you should remember when you meditate.

Different people define meditation in various ways. There is no right and wrong way to describe it. Simply put, meditation is what you make it. For some people, meditation is simply a way to silence the mind, while others see it as a way to achieve enlightenment. Some people consider meditation to be a form of prayer. To realize what meditation really is, then the best and only way to do so is to practice it on a regular basis. It should be noted that regular practice of meditation is extremely important. If you just do it once or twice a week, you will not experience its full benefits, and you will not be able to appreciate it completely. As for being an empath, meditation is a way for you to have more control of yourself and your ability. It is also an effective way to develop your empathic ability and gain mastery over it. Indeed, if you are serious about learning more and controlling your ability, then regularly practicing meditation is a must.

Before we move on to the ways you can practice meditation, let us first cover some basic guidelines. If you want to start meditating, the first thing that you want to learn is the proper posture for meditation. Now, there are many ways to meditate. You can do it while lying down, sitting, standing, or even while moving (example: walking). However, for purposes of the meditation techniques in this book, it is suggested that you meditate in a sitting position. The standing position can prevent you from falling asleep, but it tends to focus on your physical body, and it can be tiring and uncomfortable in the long run. Meditating in a lying position is good and relaxing. However, it tends to make you fall asleep. Meditating while moving, on the other hand, prevents you from shifting your focus away from your physical body. This is why practicing meditation in a sitting position is advised since it allows you to enjoy the benefits of being able to relax while at the same time, it also prevents you from falling asleep.

When you meditate, an important thing to remember is to keep your back straight. This is because the 7 main *chakras* of the body are located along the spine. To aid the free and smooth flow of energy in the body, you have to keep your spine straight.

While you meditate, you will be surprised just how your thoughts easily jump at random. Only a few people pay attention to the behavior of their thoughts, so you will probably be surprised how your thoughts change quickly and almost uncontrollably. Do not worry, this is normal. As long as you regularly practice meditation, you will be more in control of your thoughts. In Buddhism, this is referred to as the

Chapter 3: Best Practices

'monkey mind' where the mind is like a monkey that jumps from one branch of thought to another.

By regularly practicing meditation, your mind will be calmer, and you will be able to keep it still. Do not entertain stray thoughts as they will break your concentration. However, do not force yourself to push them away as doing so will only make you think about them even more. Instead, just let go of them gently and do not give them any attention. Just gently bring your focus back to your meditation. Do not use force. If you use force, you will find it hard to relax. Be still and let go.

Now that you are well aware of the basics of meditation, it is time to move on to the ways you can practice meditation. You might want to read the instructions first to familiarize yourself. You can also make an audio recording so that you can listen to your voice as you meditate. Most of these meditation techniques are known as 'guided meditations,' so you can either memorize the instructions or make your own voice recording that you could listen to as you meditate. Without further ado, listed below are the meditation techniques:

Meditation on the breath

This is probably the most basic form of meditation in the world. Even the great Buddha was said to have practiced this meditation, so it is definitely worth learning. In fact, many experienced meditators today also spend years doing this meditation. Its great power lies in its simplicity. It is also known as breathing meditation. The steps are as follows:

1. Assume a meditative posture and relax.

2. Now, place all of your focus on your breathing.

3. Breathe in through your nose, and then gently breathe out. If thoughts arise in your mind, do not give them any attention. Just focus on the breath. In your reality, nothing exists in your mind but the breath.

4. Breathe in, and out. Be gentle. Focus on your breathing.

5. If you want to stop, simply think about your body and will yourself back it. You can then gently open your eyes.

This is a very simple meditation technique with profound effects. Again, its power lies in its simplicity. Regular practice of this meditation develops the *chakras* in the body, including the *chakras* related to empathy.

Butterfly effect

This is an excellent meditation technique that will fill you with positive energy. In relation to empathy, this meditation will allow you to fill your heart *chakra* with happy and peaceful memories. This is a good technique to use when you are feeling down or simply want to feel happier. The steps are as follows:

Assume a meditative posture and relax.

1. Think of a happy memory. If you want, you can also come up with your own happy thought. The important

Chapter 3: Best Practices

thing is to keep the thought happy and peaceful. Relive this happy event.

2. See yourself smiling and feeling happy. You are filled with joy, love, and kindness, and you are satisfied.

3. Visualize this event happening and see and feel it with your heart. Raise your right hand and place it on your heart. Feel the joyful energy and bliss of this happy event or memory.

4. Now, think of another happy event. If you want, you can also visualize your dreams turning into reality. Feel the energy of happiness and success.

5. Pay more attention to how you feel about it than what you imagine. Remember that you are learning how to understand emotions, so be more in touch with your feelings.

6. Make the quality of the energy as pleasant as possible. Feel free to extend the meditation and think of more happy thoughts and events.

7. If you want to end the meditation, simply think of your physical body and will yourself back. You can gently open your eyes with a smile. Be happy and live happily.

If you want, you can spread the feeling and energy of bliss to your whole body. This is a good way to start healing the body, especially after you have been exposed to negative people. The key is to fill yourself with positive energy.

White light

This exercise deals more with clairvoyance than empathy. However, keep in mind that both abilities are interconnected. Just as the power of clairvoyance has to do with the third eye *chakra*, which happens to be the seat of intuition, the heart *chakra* is also related to the said third eye *chakra* (*Ajna chakra*).

While practicing this meditation, it is important that you do not fall asleep. However, if you do fall asleep, do not be hard on yourself. It simply means that you need to rest. To avoid falling asleep, it is best to do this in the morning just after you wake up. Also, for this meditation, it is advised that you assume a lying position. The steps are as follows:

1. Close your eyes and relax.

2. Breathe in gently and breathe out. As you breathe in, think and feel positive energy entering your system.

3. As you breathe out, feel all the day's stress being released from of your body.

4. Once you are feeling more relaxed, just be still and think of nothing. Now, focus on the light.

5. With your eyes closed, consider everything that you see, that isn't black, to be light.

6. Focus on this light. After some time, visions will start to emerge. Just relax and go with it.

Chapter 3: Best Practices

7. You will probably feel sleepy once you reach this part, but you must stop yourself from falling asleep.

8. You can allow your body to fall asleep, but your mind should remain conscious at all times. Focus on the vision, relax, and let go.

Connect

This meditation is a good way to connect to another person. If you are just starting out, you should first connect with a single person only. Before you meet with that person, it is advised that you spend some time alone with yourself and practice introspection. This will help you notice the changes caused by an external force. This is a good exercise to learn how to use your ability in a practical manner. It will allow you to connect with another person, so you can understand him or her more effectively. This is not really a meditation but more of a technique that you can use in your day-to-day life. The steps are as follows:

1. Talk with someone, preferably, someone who has a positive nature.

2. Now, imagine a cord of energy extending from your heart and connect it to the heart *chakra* of the person you are talking with.

3. Visualize this energy cord as a link between you and them. Through this link, let both of your emotions flow.

4. See and feel the emotions of your partner flowing through this cord. How does it make you feel?

The Enlightened Empath

5. Regularly practicing this exercise will let you know what another person is feeling even without engaging in actual conversation. Pay attention to how your feelings change as you connect with the person.

6. If you want to end the exercise, simply visualize the energy cord slowly fading away.

Once you get good at this exercise, you can quickly connect with anyone, and you will be able to feel and understand them easily. It is important that you do not force yourself to feel the emotion that you want or prefer. Also, do not be too attached to it. Otherwise, you might get confused with which feeling comes genuinely from you and the emotion that comes from another person. Do not expose yourself to things that are more than what you can handle.

Blessing and forgiveness

It is true that in life you cannot always choose the quality of energy that you encounter. However, you can choose how to face the challenges along the way. As an empath, you should cling to positive energy, and you should always take a positive approach. This meditation technique focuses on giving blessings to those whom you love and forgiveness to those who have offended you. This exercise will fill you with positive energy. After all, the best way to be filled with positivity is to do positive things. Here are the steps:

1. Assume a meditative posture. Close your eyes and relax.

2. Think of someone you want to bless. Raise your hands with your palms facing outward.

Chapter 3: Best Practices

3. Visualize the person whom you want to bless standing in front of you. Now, imagine a white divine light of blessing extending from your palms to the person in front of you. It is the energy of blessing.

4. Fill the person you're thinking of with love and kindness. As you do, you have to feel it in your heart.

This exercise should not be carried with a careless application of the instructions. You also need to feel it with your heart. Once you are satisfied with the blessing that you have given, you can end the exercise.

Now, for the part about forgiving, the steps are as follows:

1. Visualize the person who has offended you standing in front of you.

2. Again, raise your hands with your palms facing outward in the blessing position.

3. Now, see a white ray of light of forgiveness pouring from your hands to the person in front of you.

4. Silently state the name of the person, and say, "I forgive you." Continue to shower him or her with the energy of forgiveness.

5. Feel yourself giving forgiveness. Take note that the person does not need to actually ask you for forgiveness. Forgiveness is free, and it is for everyone. You can give it to anyone at any time. Forgive and let go.

6. If you want to end the exercise, simply visualize the ray of light and the person in front of you slowly fading away. End the exercise with the words, "I forgive you." Slowly, open your eyes with a smile.

This is a wonderful technique for emotional healing. Most of the time, the things that wound you and make you feel bad is actually the hatred or anger that you keep inside you. By forgiving the people who have hurt you, you will be able to show kindness towards yourself to let go of negative energies. If you do this exercise, be sure to do it sincerely.

Waterfall technique

This is an effective cleansing technique that you can do, especially after spending time with a negative person. Cleansing is required to rid yourself of negative energy that has attached itself to you. If you want some quick emotional healing, then this technique is quite helpful in that regard. The more that you practice this meditation, the more that you will get good at it. The steps are as follows:

1. Assume a meditative posture and relax.

2. Close your eyes and visualize bathing in a waterfall. Feel the power of the water cleansing you, removing all negative energies that have been attached to you.

3. See and feel yourself shining brighter and brighter as you get cleansed by the water.

4. Do not rush this exercise. Do not stop until you are convinced that you are fully cleansed of negativity.

5. See and feel the water brushing away all negative energies. You are now shining, full of light and power.

6. If you want to end the exercise, simply think of your physical body and will yourself back.

Bubble shield

This is an important meditation technique that you should definitely learn if you are an empath. This is a basic protective measure used by psychics. It is a must for empaths. This technique creates a bubble of energy around you that blocks all negative energies and emotions. The steps are as follows:

1. Assume a meditative posture.

2. Close your eyes and relax.

3. Visualize a strong bubble of energy around your body.

4. Now, see and feel a divine light coming from the sky charging this bubble of energy.

5. Let it continue to charge your bubble of energy, making it stronger every second.

6. Silently, or out loud, say: "This bubble shield protects me from all negative energies and emotions."

7. Continue to charge the bubble shield as much as you want.

8. Once you feel satisfied, simply visualize that the ray of light is slowly fading away.

The power of your bubble shield will weaken over time. A well-charged shield can last for about 24 hours. If you feel your shield becoming weak, just recharge it again with energy using the ray of light. If you know that you will be dealing with a difficult person or if you will be facing a crowd of them, I suggest that you prepare for it by creating a bubble shield.

Sensing

This is not completely a meditation exercise, but it is something that you can do as you go about your day. The way to do this is pretty simple and straightforward. However, it will probably take some time before you get the hang of it. The steps are as follows:

1. Look around you and choose a person to connect to.

2. As usual, send a link (cord) that extends from your heart *chakra* to the heart *chakra* of the said person.

3. Now, once the imaginary link or cord is connected, think of nothing. Just keep your mind blank but remain open to ideas and thoughts. Soon, images and emotions will arise.

4. Try to check if they gave you the correct idea about the person by talking to the person and see how he or she responds to you. Once you get good at this exercise, you will be able to sense anyone and find out their present state of mind or state of feeling.

Just like the other exercises in this book, this exercise also requires continuous practice.

Mindfulness

An empath must learn how to be mindful. Unfortunately, most people these days are unconscious of the present moment. They focus on the past and the future so much that they fail to fully experience the present moment. As an empath, you have to be mindful of the present moment. Mindfulness is about fully experiencing life and living in the present. This may surprise you, but more than 90% of people are not completely conscious of the present. This is why people barely notice the details of the outfit of the person whom they just talked to a few minutes ago. They may not even know how the handle of the door feels like when they opened it. Since you are an empath, keep in mind that you need to be mindful. Here are some exercises that will teach you mindfulness:

- When you talk with someone, be sure to listen attentively to what the other person is saying. Make a conscious effort to really listen and understand the person.

- As you walk, feel the earth beneath your feet with every step. When you breathe, feel the air enter and leave your body. Feel and be aware of what goes on around you.

- When you open the door, feel the knob in your hand.

- If everything seems to be confusing, just stop and observe what goes on around you. Take a deep breath, observe, and be still.

You are free to come up with your own exercises to instill mindfulness. The important thing to remember is that you must always be aware and be in the present moment. Another important thing to take note of is to keep track of how you are feeling. Keep in mind that empathy is about feelings, so you need to keep your emotions in check. Try to discern if what you are feeling comes from you or something that you sense outside of you (other people). Be mindful and be conscious of what goes on around you.

Yoga

Yoga is another excellent way to relax, relieve yourself of stress, as well as to develop your empathic ability. In the modern world, yoga is marketed merely as a way to release stress. However, if you take a closer look, you will find out that yoga goes far beyond a method of relaxation and removing stress. In fact, it is a rich spiritual practice that dates back to ancient times.

You do not have to be a certified yoga instructor to practice yoga. Although enrolling in a formal yoga class can help, you can still practice yoga on your own in the comfort of your home. Thanks to technology, there are many videos and articles online that you can use to learn at least the basics of yoga.

With just a simple search online, you can learn about the different yoga poses and exercises that you can try at home. Just like meditation, you need to practice yoga on a regular basis to get the most out of it. Also, the practice of meditation

Chapter 3: Best Practices

is an important part of yoga. In fact, some people believe that the whole practice of yoga is one complete meditation.

Before you start practicing yoga, you might want to invest in a good-quality yoga mat. You can easily find this by visiting sports stores or online shops. Yoga is becoming so popular these days, so you can easily find the things you need by visiting a store.

The next thing you want to do is to learn the different poses. Now, a common mistake committed by beginners is to try learning everything at once. This is not the suggested method as you might end up not remembering anything. What you want to do is to learn at least two or three poses every day. Focus more on quality than quantity. It is better if you can execute a single pose perfectly than doing five poses poorly. Do not worry, if you decide to practice yoga then you will most likely practice it daily, so there's no need to rush the development and learning process.

You might be surprised just how effective yoga can be. The benefits of yoga can be experienced on the physical, mental, emotional, and even on the spiritual level. Practicing the different poses regularly is key to attaining success. Of course, this is not just about the physical movements. Another important thing to take note of is feeling the movements and the flow of energy in the body. You will soon realize that empathy is not just about feelings and emotions, but it also includes being sensitive to all kinds and forms of subtle energy all around you. However, before you can reach this level of realization, you must first grow and mature in your knowledge and practice of being an empath.

Relaxation

As an empath, learning how to relax is considered very important. If you fail to control yourself and relax, then you will most likely make the mistake of being controlled by other people's emotions. Therefore, as an empath, it is important for you to learn how to relax and calm yourself as much as possible. If you are not relaxed, then you will not be able to control yourself and your ability.

Now, being relaxed is not difficult. However, it can be a challenge to relax if you're around things that put pressure on you. For example, how can you relax if you are conversing with a difficult person who's offensive and rude? There are different ways to relax, and not losing control is key. The more relaxed you are, then the more you are in control of the situation. Of course, there are obvious things that you can do to relax, such as exercising, having a massage, practicing meditation, and yoga, among others.

However, how can you relax if you are confronted with a difficult situation? The secret is not to be attached to it. A good way to do this is to delay taking any action or response. By simply delaying your response, you can have more control of yourself and the situation. For example, if someone offends you and you feel like retaliating negatively, just resist taking any action.

Instead, you should just let time pass by. Sooner or later, you will notice that you are no longer that offended and that you can react properly. Many times, people do not respond to situations the way they really wanted. If only they could delay their response a little bit, then maybe they could have taken a

Chapter 3: Best Practices

better course of action. As an empath, you need more time to respond since you have to discern which emotions are genuinely your own and which of them belong to others. Make sure that you decide based on your own emotion or feelings and not because you were merely swayed by other people's feelings. Again, this is another reason why you should practice introspection regularly so that you could identify your own feelings from the rest.

For empaths, one of the best ways to relax is simply to spend some time alone. You do not need to go the desert or a mountain to do this. If you do not want to travel, you can just enjoy some alone time in your room. The important thing is that you're alone, and there's no one around to distract you. Indeed, solitude is important for empaths.

Another important thing to learn is that relaxation is also a state of mind. Even if you go to a solemn place, you can find it hard to relax if your mind is filled with negative thoughts. If you want to relax, then you should either fill your mind with positive thoughts or keep it still. Never entertain a negative thought. More importantly, do not worry about anything. Worrying only makes you face the same problem twice, and it is not good for your state of mind. As the Buddhist saying goes, "If you can solve your problem, what is the use of worrying? If you cannot solve your problem, what is the use of worrying?" The lesson here is simple, stop worrying so much about everything.

True relaxation affects us on all levels: physical, mental, emotional, and spiritual. Meditation and the practice of yoga are excellent ways to relax. However, you do not need to make things complicated. If you want, you can just simply lie down in bed and drink a glass of fresh juice. Relaxing is not hard, and it will allow you to think more clearly and effectively. Any moment that you realize that you are not relaxed and that you are feeling pressured, just stop and gently bring yourself back to a state of relaxation. As an empath, emotions and subtle energies have a strong impact on you. Therefore, you need to learn how to stay in control of yourself and the situation. The only way for you to stay in control is to stay relaxed so that you can be calm enough to handle things more effectively.

Remember that no matter how much negativity surrounds you, it cannot overcome you without your consent. What you need to do is to detach yourself from everything, so that you will not be strongly affected. This is true especially if you are stuck in a difficult situation.

To relax, you need to free yourself from negative energies. Now, a common mistake is to try to free one's self from negativity by thinking too much about negative things. Do not think, "I should remove the negative energies." Instead, you should take a more positive approach and say, "I am filling myself and my life with pure positive energies." Remember that the more than you think or acknowledge negativity, the stronger it will be. So, the more effective approach is simply to focus on the opposite. Just be positive, and the negativity will disappear on its own.

If you find it impossible to relax, then it only means that you have exposed yourself to energy that is more than you can handle at the present time. If this happens, you should retreat and spend time alone in quiet contemplation. This is not a sign

Chapter 3: Best Practices

of weakness, this is normal, for empaths who are still learning to control their ability. Do not worry, this is only temporary. Once you get better control over your ability, you will no longer have to retreat from any situation. However, since you are just starting out, it is best that you know when to take a step back and take a deep breath.

Being an empath is not about being too overwhelmed by strong emotions. Yes, you can expect to face many different emotions, but you should not allow these emotions to influence you so much that it ends up controlling your actions. Do not forget that you always have a choice. Make sure that you are relaxed. If you are not relaxed, then that is a sign that you are probably starting to lose control because of other people's emotions and energies. However, as long as you can relax, then you will stay in control.

Chapter 4: Do's and Don'ts

Dos

Write a journal

Although this is not considered a requirement, it is strongly advised that you try it just once. Writing a personal journal or diary can be very helpful for empaths. It will allow you to see yourself from a much better perspective, from a standpoint that is free from any form of bias and prejudice. Now, you do not need to be a professional writer to keep a journal. You simply have to update it regularly and be completely honest with everything that you write in your journal. You can write everything that you want in your journal that is related to your empathic ability. Ideally, your journal should include your honest feelings and opinions regarding your empathic ability, as well as your goals. And don't forget to write down the actual steps that you are taking to gain mastery over your ability. You should take note of your strengths and weaknesses. Also, you should further improve your strengths and work on your weaknesses. Keep in mind that there is no end to self-improvement.

Now, some people want to start writing a journal but are not fond of writing. In this case, you might want to use a file on your computer or even a writing application on your mobile phone. You do not need to write in a notebook. The important thing is to have a place where you can keep all your thoughts and be able to update them whenever you want.

In the first few weeks, you might not appreciate the beauty of having a journal or diary. However, just persist in your practice and in updating your journal. After some time, you will soon appreciate having a journal, especially once you start to see your progress.

Having a journal is also an excellent way to identify your strengths and weaknesses more easily. Just be sure that once you notice these things, you should work on them immediately.

Take note that you do not need to make your journal complicated. In fact, if you want, you can even write everything down in bullet points. The important thing is to record what happens on your journey. Needless to say, you should also make it a habit to read your journal and to make reflections every now and then. Pay attention to any new lessons that you might encounter along the way. Do not forget that this is precisely what the journal is for. It should help you learn more about being an empath. Again, it is extremely important to be very honest with every little thing that you put in your journal. Unfortunately, some people only want to record their strengths and turn a blind eye to their weaknesses. This won't help since it prevents you from achieving more progress. The more that you accept and acknowledge your weaknesses, the more you can improve since you will know exactly what to work on.

Chapter 4: Do's and Don'ts

Mingle with positive people

As an empath, you have a special connection with the people around you. Now, this can be a problem if you are surrounded by negative people. Even for non-empaths, it is not easy to deal with negative people. You do not have to make your life difficult. As much as you can, surround yourself with positive people. You are probably familiar with the saying, "You are the average of the five people around you." This saying only shows how much the people you mingle with have an effect on you. Of course, it's up to you if you will allow yourself to be influenced by others, but it does not change the fact that the people you mingle with, especially on a regular basis, have a significant effect on you. This is why you should try to mingle only with positive people. This way, you will avoid negative energies easily. Empaths are even more sensitive when they get exposed to negativity, which is why you should at least lessen your exposure to negative energies by choosing the people you want to spend time with.

Positive people are those who make you feel good about yourself, and you feel alive being around them. They are the ones who give you strength and courage during difficult times. Take note that positive people are not perfect people. They also have their own faults and imperfections. However, unlike negative people, you feel better when you are with them, and they bring out the best in you.

Of course, you cannot expect that life is full of positive people. From time to time, you will have to deal with difficult people. Difficult people make the presence of positive people in your life even more special. A common mistake is to take the positive people in our life for granted. As an empath, you should be sensitive enough to feel and remind yourself of their importance in your life.

It is also much easier to use empathy and connect with a positive person than a negative person. This is because you have the natural willingness to connect and understand the person on a deeper level. This willingness plays an important role in making an ideal connection. If you honestly do not want to connect to another, then you will have a wall that will divide the relationship. If you mingle with positive people, it becomes natural for you to be more open and to make a connection. However, even if you are surrounded by positive people, you should not forget your own identity.

Continuous practice

You cannot just drop or forget about your ability. You should realize that being an empath requires continuous practice. Otherwise, your ability might end up controlling you. You need to make use of your ability. Otherwise, it will be nothing more than a burden. To ensure that you will stay in control, you have to continuously practice the exercises in this book, as well as other exercises that you may have learned elsewhere or on your own.

Now, many people have an erroneous idea of continuous practice. So, what exactly does it mean? True practice is about making it a part of your life. Simply put, you have to live the teachings. Do not think of the practice of meditation and others to be some kind of work that you hate. Rather, you should try to enjoy them as they should now be a natural part of your life. Continuous practice can help you accept the truth

Chapter 4: Do's and Don'ts

that you are an empath, and you must live your life as a true empath.

Now, you might think that this is tiring. Well, once you fully realize and accept your gift of empathy, then you will no longer see this as a form of practice. What's important is that you should make empathy a way of life. The best practice is applying and living your gift. It is not something that you use today and forgets about the next day. Once you realize that this is a way of life instead of a mere 'practice,' then the more you can embrace your gift and accept it. This is why successful empaths do not get tired of their ability. This is because they have accepted their gift and have decided to live with it.

If at some point, you start feeling tired with the practices, take some time to realize that the practices are not just tools that you resort to, but they are now a part of your life. Realize that you are an empath, and that empathy is a natural part of you. Since you cannot escape it no matter how hard you try, then you should live in harmony with it. Continuous practice is about living your life in harmony with your ability.

Positive thinking

Positive thinking is very important for empaths, otherwise, you can be easily overcome by negative emotions and energies. However, you should understand that there is a difference between positive thinking and fooling yourself. Positive thinking does not mean that you no longer recognize the presence of negative energies in your life. It is not a self-deluding approach. Rather, it is more about choosing to face the challenges in life with a positive attitude.

The Enlightened Empath

Your mind is very powerful, which is why you should be careful with the thoughts that you entertain. Take note that it is not just having thoughts that matter, but it is also important that you pay close attention to the quality of your thoughts.

The thing is that even when negative emotions attach themselves to you, you have the power to choose how you will respond to it. Even if you are in a crowd of negative and difficult people, it is up to you how you will react to it. If you think negatively, then you will most likely end up being controlled by others. However, if you remain positive, then you will know that you are still in complete control of yourself.

External forces can only influence you and make suggestions, but everything still depends on what you will choose to do. Of course, you only act according to your state of mind. To make sure that you will choose the right course of action, you should keep your mind positive.

Again, positive thinking is not wishful thinking. Rather, it is about seeing things from a better perspective. Is the cup half full or half empty? In life, problems will always come and how you will handle these problems depends on you. Will you see them as mere stumbling blocks or stepping stones that lead to a much happier and meaningful life? Or, will you see problems as a wall you have no chance of climbing over and just give up?

Although you may not always have the option to choose what happens in your life, you can always choose how you want to live your life despite what happens to everything around you. It is true that you have almost no control over external things, but you can exercise control and mastery over your mind. If you have empathic abilities, then you need to be at peace with your mind. You cannot have peace of mind if you continue to have thoughts thick with negativity. You must strive to fill your mind only with positive things, or at least positively view things.

Sometimes the best thing to do is simply to ignore negative things. Indeed, some of the thoughts that you have in your mind are just plain noise. If you ignore them, they'll disappear on their own. Just be very careful with the thoughts that you entertain, and keep your thoughts positive to live a good life.

Know who you are

As an empath, it is important that you have a clear understanding of who you are. Otherwise, it will be easy for you to be controlled by other people's emotions. When it comes to knowing one's self better, you have to do a great deal of introspection. This is not a problem once you understand that being an empath is a way of life and not just a set of practices that you must do.

However, truly knowing one's self is not that simple. Most people don't just have wrong ideas about themselves, but they also refuse to see their real selves. This usually happens when you refuse to acknowledge your weaknesses and imperfections. This is why it's important that you learn to be humble and honest with yourself. In fact, you should be surprised if you do not see any weaknesses. It only means that you need to look more closely. Once you have a better understanding of who you are, then the more easily you can deal with issues relating to empathy.

You do not need to be a person without a weakness. That would be hard, if not impossible. However, you can choose what your weaknesses would be. What's important is that you will further develop your strengths and work on your weaknesses. Again, always keep an eye on continuous improvement.

If you want to try learning more about yourself, you need to possess an unbiased and unprejudiced mind. You need to see things as they truly are. Remember that the more that you are being honest with yourself, the better. Empathy is not about feeling what you want to feel, but it should show you reality. Of course, there are things you can do to twist your perception of reality into what you prefer, but you should not expect this to work all of the time. Once you know more about yourself, then you will also know the things or qualities that you need to work on. The only thing that is left for you to do is to take action.

Take a break

Practicing your empathic ability can be fun. However, it can also be tiring, especially in the long run. Taking a break every now and then is highly recommended so you won't burn yourself out. When you take a break, do not be like other people who still worry about how they need to gain mastery over their ability as soon as possible. That is not taking a break. When you take a break, you should not even think about your ability. Use that opportunity to fully relax and just enjoy life. After taking a break, you will have to work on gaining control of your ability again, and you are expected to exert more effort. Now, do not use this as an excuse for being lazy. Take note that you should only give yourself a break only if you deserve it. This means that you should some results first before you take a break.

Don'ts

Do not lie to yourself

Lying to yourself will not help you in any way. In fact, it will only lead to you misunderstanding yourself. Most of the time, people lie to themselves when they do not like reality. You should understand that when you work with your empathic ability, you need to deal with reality as it is and not how you want it to be. Don't worry, once you gain a better understanding of the situation, the more easily you can turn it into something that you prefer. However, when you lie to yourself, then you lose any chance at further developing your ability.

You need to keep an open and honest mind. Do not judge yourself but only see things as they truly are. The same is true whenever you try to understand a particular emotion. Accept and feel the emotion concerned without adding your own opinions. By keeping an open mind and taking things just as they are, you will be able to understand yourself more easily.

Now, it is not easy to be honest with yourself, especially when you have to deal with your own weaknesses. And every time that you feel like you're lying to yourself, take that as a reminder that you should be more honest about what you really think and feel. Well-experienced empaths know that, when it comes to understanding emotions that they feel, they need to be calm and honest. You cannot impose what you want to feel versus what you really feel. Indeed, to grow as an empath, you need to keep an open mind.

The moment that you lie to yourself is the moment when you get misdirected. This is wrong as it does not only waste your time, but it further deludes you and prevents you from really knowing yourself.

Instead of lying to yourself, you should acknowledge your weaknesses. Take note that this does not mean that you merely accept your weaknesses as they are. Rather, you should be ready to change them.

After all, you cannot work on your weaknesses unless you are aware that they exist. At any point that you realize that you have lied to yourself, correct it right away. The more honest you are, the more that you will understand yourself and your ability.

Forget about everything that you know about yourself. If you just started working on your empathic ability, then it is better to begin with a clean slate. So, drop all the misconceptions that you have about yourself and start anew.

Even if you're just discerning the energy that you sense from other people, you should exercise an open mind. Remember that reality may not always be the way you want it to be. Do not change or edit the impressions as you sense them, but take them simply as they are. Although you may misunderstand them in the beginning, you will soon get the hang of it. You just have to persist in your practice, and you mustn't forget to be honest with yourself.

Chapter 4: Do's and Don'ts

Do not give up

Having mastery over your ability takes time and effort. Even if you read lots of books on the subject, it does not mean that you will immediately have control of your ability. Just like learning any other skill, taking control of your empathic ability requires time, effort, and continuous practice.

In trying to take control of your ability, there will be times that you will feel frustrated. Sometimes, no matter how hard you try, you will be overwhelmed by other people's emotions. If this ever happens to you (and it most probably will), do not be discouraged. The more that you practice your ability, the better you will get at controlling it. The important thing is not to give up. So, just continue with your practices. Learning to control your ability really takes a lot of time and effort. In fact, it usually takes more than a month of continuous practice to learn how you can control your empathic ability. You must learn from every mistake, and then make appropriate adjustments to avoid committing the same and similar mistakes in the future.

Again, you should not entertain negative thoughts like saying you cannot do it. You need to think positively. If you ever feel like giving up, try not to entertain that thought and just take a break. Sometimes all you need is a good rest to get you back in the game. The important thing is not to give up. Remember that as long as you keep on trying, you will never lose.

If you want to gain mastery over your ability, you should expect to face hardships and challenges. After all, everything that is worth having has its own challenges. Do not feel bad about having to face obstacles along the way, as this will teach you the important lessons that you need to learn to succeed and achieve your goals.

Expect that once you start gaining control over your ability, you will be put to the test. However, just keep in mind that you have the power that you need to succeed. It is all a matter of doing and actually getting things right. So, do not give up and stay strong no matter what.

Successful empaths have their own stories to share about the difficulties that they have faced. In fact, even today, they still continue to face challenges. Once again, continuous practice means making empathy a way of life than just a mere practice that you do whenever you feel like it. Also, just think about it, why should you give up on your gift? There are many people out there who even want to be just like you. It's true that it's not easy, but nobody said that it was easy in the first place. But, if you take responsibility and place your ability under your control, that is when you will start appreciating its beauty as a blessing, and you will be able to use it for good.

Do not entertain negative thoughts

Negative thoughts and energies are the enemies of an empathic mind. They tend to make things worse. So, stay away from negativity as much as possible. However, there will be instances when you have no choice but to deal with them. In this case, the best thing to do is to think positive and view them more constructively. Consider these negative thoughts as a means to train your mind. After all, in life, you will have to face negative thoughts every now and then, and so it is only right that you get used to them and learn how to handle them effectively.

Chapter 4: Do's and Don'ts

Now, a common mistake is simply to tell yourself to not think or entertain negative thoughts. You have to understand that this is not enough. Even if you dismiss negative thoughts, then you will be left with nothing, and since the last thought that you have is a negative thought, then there is a chance that it will be followed by another negative thought.

So, what should you do? The best approach is to do the opposite. Instead of just dismissing negative thoughts as they arise in your mind, you should think of positive thoughts. As you can see, it is not a matter of removing negative thoughts but more about changing the degree. According to an ancient teaching, opposites are the same, they just differ in degree. So, when you encounter negative thoughts, instead of trying so hard to push them away, simply focus on the opposite and start filling your mind with positive thoughts.

As an empath, your state of mind is very important. If your mind is full of negative thoughts, then you will most likely feel bad. However, if your mind is filled with positive thoughts, then you will also feel good and happy. It is important for you to understand that although you do not have complete control over a lot of things, you can still exercise control over your own mind. This is a key element when it comes to dealing with your ability, as your own feelings are greatly influenced by your state of mind. It is wrong to think that one's feelings are not connected to the mind. This is because the mind affects everything. It is also what you use to take control of your emotions and feelings. Hence, to have mastery of your ability, then you also need to gain mastery over your mind. Once again, the exercises in this book, especially the meditation techniques, are the best tools that you can use to achieve mastery over your mind.

Do not let people change who you are

This is one of the most common challenges that empaths deal with. This is true especially if you do not take the time and effort to learn and gain control of your ability. The tendency is that you will be overcome by other people's emotions to the point that you can no longer discern their emotions from your own. When this happens, you become a product of their emotions and feelings. This, of course, has a strong impact on your life.

Although this may not be much of a problem if you are exposed to positive energies, you know that life is not always full of positive things. Indeed, you will have to deal with some negative forces along the way.

This is why doing introspection is very important. You should never lose your self-identity. The moment that you feel that you are being exposed to an energy that is more than that you can handle, you should take a step back. If you cannot avoid the situation, then that is a good time for you to cast a bubble shield or at least cleanse your mind. If you are in a public environment, then you might want to go to the restroom for a few minutes to do at least one of the meditation techniques.

Although it is suggested that you meditate in a sitting position, the meditation techniques in this book can also be done while standing and even without closing your eyes. If you get good at them, you can even meditate discreetly in a public place.

Chapter 4: Do's and Don'ts

Do not think of your ability as a curse

Never think of your empathic ability as a curse. Rather, it is a gift that you should use and cherish. In the beginning, you might see it as a curse only because you do not know how to use it properly yet. This can be likened to a knife. If you do not know how to use a knife, it can wound and hurt you. However, once you learn how to use it, then you can use it to cook food and do many other wonderful things. Your empathic ability is what you make it. It can be a curse if you do not take control of it, but it can be a blessing once you finally learn to control it. In fact, you do not even need to attain mastery just to appreciate your ability as a gift.

If you stick to the exercises in this book, you will soon start to appreciate the beauty of what you have in just a few weeks of practice. Just be sure to do the exercises properly.

By now, you should already understand that what you have is a gift, a blessing. It is up to you to use it by being helpful to others. Keep in mind that your ability is not something that you should use to abuse or violate the rights and privacy of others. Instead, it is meant to be shared in a mutual way, in a manner that will help people and build ideal relationships. Remember, the true meaning of empathy depends on how you use it.

Conclusion

Thanks for making it through to the end of this book. We hope it was informative and that it provided you with all of the tools you need to achieve your goals whatever they may be.

The next step is to apply everything that you have learned and start taking control over your empathic ability. In the beginning, you will definitely encounter challenges. But do not worry, if you practice persistently, you will get better and have total control over your ability soon enough. The important thing is to keep on trying and never give up.

You have a gift. It is up to you to learn more about it and to wield it effectively. This book has given you the knowledge that you need, it is your job, to put your newfound knowledge into actual practice.

Finally, if you found this book useful in any way, a review on Amazon is always appreciated!

Lightning Source UK Ltd.
Milton Keynes UK
UKHW021858191219
355693UK00015B/365/P